1939 U.K.

YEARBOOK

ISBN: 9781790291274

This book gives a fascinating and informative insight into life in the United Kingdom in 1939. It includes everything from the most popular music of the year to the cost of a buying a new house. Additionally, there are chapters covering people in high office, the best-selling films of the year and all the main news and events. Want to know which team won the FA Cup or which British personalities were born in 1939? All this and much more awaits you within.

INDEX

FIRST EDITION

1939

January

M	T	W	T	F	S	S
						1
2	3	4	5	6	7	8
9	10	11	12	13	14	15
16	17	18	19	20	21	22
23	24	25	26	27	28	29
30	31					

○:5 ◑:12 ●:20 ◐:28

February

M	T	W	T	F	S	S
		1	2	3	4	5
6	7	8	9	10	11	12
13	14	15	16	17	18	19
20	21	22	23	24	25	26
27	28					

○:4 ◑:11 ●:19 ◐:27

March

M	T	W	T	F	S	S
		1	2	3	4	5
6	7	8	9	10	11	12
13	14	15	16	17	18	19
20	21	22	23	24	25	26
27	28	29	30	31		

○:5 ◑:12 ●:21 ◐:28

April

M	T	W	T	F	S	S
					1	2
3	4	5	6	7	8	9
10	11	12	13	14	15	16
17	18	19	20	21	22	23
24	25	26	27	28	29	30

○:4 ◑:11 ●:19 ◐:26

May

M	T	W	T	F	S	S
1	2	3	4	5	6	7
8	9	10	11	12	13	14
15	16	17	18	19	20	21
22	23	24	25	26	27	28
29	30	31				

○:3 ◑:11 ●:19 ◐:26

June

M	T	W	T	F	S	S
			1	2	3	4
5	6	7	8	9	10	11
12	13	14	15	16	17	18
19	20	21	22	23	24	25
26	27	28	29	30		

○:2 ◑:10 ●:17 ◐:24

July

M	T	W	T	F	S	S
					1	2
3	4	5	6	7	8	9
10	11	12	13	14	15	16
17	18	19	20	21	22	23
24	25	26	27	28	29	30
31						

○:1 ◑:9 ●:16 ◐:23 ○:31

August

M	T	W	T	F	S	S
	1	2	3	4	5	6
7	8	9	10	11	12	13
14	15	16	17	18	19	20
21	22	23	24	25	26	27
28	29	30	31			

◑:8 ●:15 ◐:21 ○:29

September

M	T	W	T	F	S	S
				1	2	3
4	5	6	7	8	9	10
11	12	13	14	15	16	17
18	19	20	21	22	23	24
25	26	27	28	29	30	

◑:6 ●:13 ◐:20 ○:28

October

M	T	W	T	F	S	S
						1
2	3	4	5	6	7	8
9	10	11	12	13	14	15
16	17	18	19	20	21	22
23	24	25	26	27	28	29
30	31					

◑:6 ●:12 ◐:20 ○:28

November

M	T	W	T	F	S	S
		1	2	3	4	5
6	7	8	9	10	11	12
13	14	15	16	17	18	19
20	21	22	23	24	25	26
27	28	29	30			

◑:4 ●:11 ◐:19 ○:26

December

M	T	W	T	F	S	S
				1	2	3
4	5	6	7	8	9	10
11	12	13	14	15	16	17
18	19	20	21	22	23	24
25	26	27	28	29	30	31

◑:3 ●:10 ◐:18 ○:26

PEOPLE IN HIGH OFFICE

Monarch - King George VI
Reign: 11th December 1936 - 6th February 1952
Predecessor: Edward VIII
Successor: Elizabeth II

Prime Minister

Neville Chamberlain
Conservative Party
28th May 1937 - 10th May 1940

Ireland

Canada

United States

Taoiseach Of Ireland
Éamon de Valera
Fianna Fáil
29th December 1937
- 18th February 1948

Prime Minister
Mackenzie King
Liberal Party
23rd October 1935
- 15th November 1948

President
Franklin D. Roosevelt
Democratic Party
4th March 1933
- 12th April 1945

 Australia

Prime Minister
Joseph Lyons (1932-1939)
Sir Earle Page (1939)
Robert Menzies (1939-1941)

 Brazil

President
Getúlio Vargas (1930-1945)

 China

Premier
Kung Hsiang-his (1938-1939)
Chiang Kai-shek (1939-1945)

 Cuba

President
Federico Laredo Brú (1936-1940)

 Egypt

Prime Minister
Muhammad Mahmoud Pasha (1937-1939)
Aly Maher Pasha (1939-1940)

 France

President
Albert François Lebrun (1932-1940)

 Germany

Chancellor
Adolf Hitler (1933-1945)

 India

Viceroy of India
Victor Alexander John Hope (1936-1943)

 Italy

Prime Minister
Benito Mussolini (1922-1943)

 Japan

Prime Minister
Prince Fumimaro Konoe (1937-1939)
Baron Hiranuma Kiichirō (1939)
Nobuyuki Abe (1939-1940)

 Mexico

President
Lázaro Cárdenas (1934-1940)

 New Zealand

Prime Minister
Michael Joseph Savage (1935-1940)

 Russia

Communist Party Leader
Joseph Stalin (1922-1952)

 South Africa

Prime Minister
J. B. M. Hertzog (1924-1939)
Jan Smuts (1939-1948)

 Spain

Prime Minister
Francisco Franco (1938-1973)

 Turkey

Prime Minister
Celâl Bayar (1937-1939)
Refik Saydam (1939-1942)

BRITISH NEWS & EVENTS

JAN

2nd   The all-time highest attendance for a football league game is recorded as 118,730 people watch Rangers beat Celtic 2-1 at Ibrox Park in Glasgow.

3rd   Michael Taylor, a case maker for the British & American Tobacco Co., acts as midwife to deliver his 13th child at Salisbury Road in Liverpool. The baby, who has been named Lucky and was not due for another 2-3 weeks, weighed in at 15lb.

FEB

4th   The Irish Republican Army (IRA) bombs Tottenham Court Road and Leicester Square London Underground stations. They used timed suitcase bombs, stored in the left-luggage rooms overnight, to carry out the attacks. Two people were wounded and severe damage was done to the stations.

9th   Two further IRA bombs explode at King's Cross Station, London.

25th February: The first Anderson shelter is built in a garden in Islington, London. Named after Sir John Anderson and designed in 1938 by William Paterson and Oscar Carl Kerrison, the air raid shelter was designed to accommodate up to six people. Over 1.5 million Anderson shelters were given out before the start of WW2 to people in areas that were at risk of being bombed by the Germans. The shelters were free for people who earned less than £250 per year and for those with a higher income they could be bought for £7. *(Photo 1: Air raid shelters under construction at a factory in Newport, Wales. Photo 2: A woman hangs out her laundry next to her new Anderson air raid shelter).*

27th   Borley Rectory, a Victorian house built in 1862 that gained fame as the most haunted house in England, is destroyed by a fire.

MAR

2nd   The Daily Mirror reports that in the first three weeks of the 'National Call To Service' some 371,000 men and women in Britain enrolled for some form of service.

17th   Prime Minister Neville Chamberlain, in a speech in Birmingham, declares that Hitler has wantonly shattered the peace in Europe and that Germany will bitterly regret what her government has done.

31st   Britain pledges support to Poland in the event of an invasion.

APR

4th	The Royal Armoured Corps is formed by combining mechanised regiments from the cavalry of the line with the Royal Tank Corps.
11th	The Women's Royal Naval Service (WRNS; popularly and officially known as the Wrens) is re-established - It was first formed in 1917 for the First World War and was disbanded in 1919. The WRNS included cooks, clerks, wireless telegraphists, radar plotters, weapons analysts, range assessors, electricians and air mechanics.
12th	The IRA bomb eleven public lavatories; six in London, four in Coventry and one in Birmingham.
26th	The Military Training Act 1939 is passed by Parliament and introduces conscription for all men aged 20 and 21. Those of age would be called up for six months full-time military training and then transferred to the Reserve.

MAY

May-September: The Sutton Hoo treasure, a 7th century Anglo-Saxon ship burial, is excavated near Woodbridge, Suffolk. The principal treasures, including the Sutton Hoo helmet, are presented to the British Museum by the landowner Edith Pretty. At this time it is largest ever gift from a living donor. *(Photo 1: The Anglo Saxon ship at Sutton Hoo under excavation - Photo 2: The Sutton Hoo helmet).*

6th	Dorothy Garrod, an archaeologist who specialises in the Palaeolithic period, is elected to the Disney Professorship of Archaeology at the University of Cambridge. She is the first woman to hold an Oxbridge chair.
15th	The British film Goodbye, Mr. Chips, based on the 1934 novella of the same name by James Hilton, is released. Starring Robert Donat, Greer Garson and Terry Kilburn, it was shot at Denham Studios, Buckinghamshire and at Repton School in the village of Repton in Derbyshire. Actor Robert Donat went on to win the 1939 Academy Award for Best Actor for his performance in the film.
17th	King George VI and Queen Elizabeth arrive in Quebec City to begin the first-ever visit to Canada by a reigning British sovereign. The visit lasted until the 15th June and covered every Canadian province, the Dominion of Newfoundland, and a few days in the United States.
23rd	Queen Mary's car overturns after colliding with a lorry in Putney. Her Majesty Queen Mary, who will be 72 on the 26th May, suffered bruising and shock as a result of the accident. The news was flashed to the King and Queen in Canada. The King sent a cable to his mother.

JUN

1st	The Group 1 T-class submarine HMS Thetis sinks, during trials in Liverpool Bay, with the loss of 99 lives. She was later salvaged, repaired and re-commissioned as HMS Thunderbolt. Thunderbolt served in the Atlantic and Mediterranean theatres until she was lost again (with all hands) on 14th March 1943.

7th June: King George VI and Queen Elizabeth board the Royal Train from Canada to visit Washington on the first visit to the United States by a reigning British sovereign. When they arrived at Union Station at 11am the following morning the streets were mobbed, with crowds in excess of 250,000 hoping for a glimpse of the Royal couple. *(Photo: Seated at the White House L-R Eleanor Roosevelt, George VI, Mrs Sara Roosevelt (the Presidents mother), Queen Elizabeth and President Franklin D. Roosevelt).*

14th	The Imperial Japanese Army blockades British trading settlements in the north China treaty port of Tientsin. Originating as a minor administrative dispute it escalated into a major diplomatic incident which lasted until the 20th August.
28th	The Women's Auxiliary Air Force (WAAF), the female auxiliary of the Royal Air Force, is created. At its peak strength in 1943, WAAF numbers exceeded 180,000 and had over 2,000 women enlisting every week.
30th	The Mersey Ferry stops running to Rock Ferry (an area of Birkenhead on the Wirral Peninsula).

JUL

1st	The Women's Land Army (WLA) is re-formed. Women who worked for the WLA were commonly known as Land Girls and by 1944 it had over 80,000 members. The WLA was a civilian organisation which was originally created during the First World War so women could work in agriculture and replace men called up to the military.
8th	The Pan American Airways, Boeing 314 flying boat Yankee Clipper, inaugurates the world's first heavier-than-air North Atlantic air passenger service between the United States and Britain (Southampton).
26th	The Barber Institute of Fine Arts at the University of Birmingham (designed by Robert Atkinson) is officially opened by Queen Mary.

24th	The National Gallery evacuates most of its paintings in London to Wales. The Emergency Powers (Defence) Act 1939 is passed. It enables the British Government to take up emergency powers to prosecute a war effectively.
25th	The IRA. explodes a bomb in Coventry, killing 5 and injuring 70 people. Two IRA. members are convicted of the bombing and hanged, while a third, who acknowledged planting the bomb, escaped. It was the first bombing, as a part of the IRA S-Plan campaign of bombing English cities, in which civilians were killed.
30th	The Royal Navy proceeds to war stations.

SEP

1st September - A 4-day evacuation of children from London and other major U.K. cities begins. The evacuation of civilians in Britain during the Second World War was designed to protect people, especially children, from the risks associated with the aerial bombing of cities. Operation Pied Piper, which began on 1st September 1939, officially relocated almost 3 million people. Later in the war there were further smaller waves of official evacuation and re-evacuation, such as from the south and east coasts in June 1940 when a seaborne invasion was expected, and from affected cities after the Blitz began in September 1940. Although most people were shipped to rural areas in Britain some went overseas to countries such as Canada, South Africa, Australia, New Zealand and the United States.

1st	Blackout regulations are imposed across Britain. This requires that all windows and doors should be covered at night with suitable material such as heavy curtains, cardboard or paint, to prevent the escape of any glimmer of light that might aid enemy aircraft.
1st	The BBC Home Service begins broadcasting. It was eventually renamed and became the current BBC Radio 4 in 1967.
1st	The BBC Television Service stops at 12:35pm after the broadcast of a Mickey Mouse cartoon. It is feared that the VHF waves of television would act as a perfect homing signal for guiding enemy bombers to central London. The BBC would resume its broadcasting in 1946 with the same Mickey Mouse cartoon.
3rd	Speaking on BBC Radio from 10 Downing Street, shortly after 11.00am, Prime Minister Neville Chamberlain announces that the United Kingdom has declared war on Nazi Germany following the German invasion of Poland. Twenty minutes later air raid sirens sound across London, but it turns out to be a false alarm.
3rd	The Prime Minister creates a small War Cabinet which includes Winston Churchill as First Lord of the Admiralty.
3rd	The National Service (Armed Forces) Act is passed by Parliament introducing National Service for all men aged 18 to 41.
3rd	The British liner SS Athenia becomes the first civilian casualty of the war when she is torpedoed and sunk (by German submarine U-30) between Rockall and Tory Island of the Irish coast. Of the 1,418 aboard, 98 passengers and 19 crew are killed.

3rd	In the week beginning today 400,000 pets are euthanised in preparation for food shortages during World War II. This was primarily in response to the National Air Raid Precautions Animals Committee (NARPAC) pamphlet entitled 'Advice to Animal Owners'. The pamphlet suggested moving pets from the big cities and into the countryside. It concluded with the statement that, 'If you cannot place them in the care of neighbours, it really is kindest to have them destroyed'. The pamphlet also contained an advertisement for a pistol that could be used to humanely kill pets.
4th	The first RAF Bomber Command raid of World War II take place at Wilhelmshaven, Germany. Ten Bristol Blenheims, of No.107 and No.110 Squadrons, attack units of the German fleet at low altitude only to lose half their number without achieving any significantly damaging hits.
5th	The National Registration Act is given Royal assent. The Act establishes a National Register which begins operating on the 29th September (National Registration Day), a system of identity cards, and a requirement that they must be produced on demand or presented to a police station within 48 hours.
9th	The British Expeditionary Force (BEF) crosses over to France. The BEF was established in 1938 (in readiness for war) after Nazi Germany annexed Austria in the Anschluss of March 1938 and made claims on Sudetenland in Czechoslovakia.
10th	The British submarine HMS Triton torpedoes and sinks another British submarine, HMS Oxley, believing her to be a German U-boat. This was the first Allied submarine casualty of World War II and it resulted in the deaths of 52 crew members. The truth behind the loss of Oxley was not revealed until the 1950s.
17th	The aircraft carrier HMS Courageous is torpedoed and sunk in the Western Approaches by German submarine U-29. This is the first British warship loss of the War and resulted in the deaths of 519 crew.
18th	Fascist politician William Joyce (better known as Lord Haw-Haw) begins broadcasting Nazi propaganda from studios in Berlin.
19th	The popular radio comedy show 'It's That Man Again', starring Tommy Handley, is broadcast for the first time on the BBC Home service. Known as ITMA, it would run for over 300 episodes until Handley's death in 1949.

24th September: Petrol rationing is introduced. This is then followed by the rationing of bacon, butter and sugar on the 8th January 1940. Successive ration schemes for meat, tea, jam, biscuits, breakfast cereals, cheese, eggs, lard, milk, and canned and dried fruit would also soon follow.

26th	Flying from HMS Ark Royal in the North Sea, Lieutenant B. S. McEwen of the Fleet Air Arm scores the first British victory over a German aircraft of the war by shooting down a Dornier Do18D flying boat.

OCT

1st	Call-up proclamation: All men aged 20 and 21 must register with the military authorities for National Service.
14th	HMS Royal Oak (one of five Revenge-class battleships built for the Royal Navy during the First World War) is sunk by the German submarine U-47 in Scapa Flow, Orkney Islands with the loss of 833 of its 1,234 crew.
16th	A Junkers Ju 88 is brought down into the sea by Spitfires following an attack on HMS Southampton, Edinburgh and Mohawk in the Rosyth Naval Dockyard on Firth of Forth, Scotland.
17th	Two air raids are carried out by the German Luftwaffe on elements of the Fleet at Scapa Flow in the Orkney Islands.
30th	The British battleship HMS Nelson is unsuccessfully attacked by the German submarine U-56, under the command of captain Wilhelm Zahn, off Orkney. The ship is hit by three torpedoes, none of which explode; Winston Churchill (First Lord of the Admiralty), Admiral of the Fleet Dudley Pound (First Sea Lord) and Admiral Charles Forbes (Commander-in-Chief Home Fleet) are all on board.

NOV

4th	Stewart Menzies is appointed as head of MI6, the Secret Intelligence Service (SIS). He expands wartime intelligence and counterintelligence departments and supervises codebreaking efforts at Bletchley Park, overseeing the work of cryptanalyst and mathematician Alan Turing. He remained in this post until his retirement aged 62 in 1952, having completed 43 years of continuous service in the British Army.
8th	The Venlo Incident: Two British agents of the SIS are captured by the Germans on the outskirts of the town of Venlo in the Netherlands.

23rd October: The British armed merchantman HMS Rawalpindi is sunk whilst patrolling north of the Faroe Islands. Despite being hopelessly outgunned by the German battleships Scharnhorst and Gneisenau, 60-year-old Captain Edward Coverley Kennedy of the Rawalpindi decided to fight rather than surrender. He was heard to say 'We'll fight them both, they'll sink us and that will be that. Good-bye'. The incident resulted in the loss of 238 men on board the Rawalpindi.

24th	The British Overseas Airways Corporation (BOAC) is formed with the merger of Imperial Airways and British Airways Ltd. (effective from 1st April 1940).

	The new Unemployment Assistance Board scales, which will be in force by Christmas, will give workless adults an extra shilling a week and children an extra sixpence. A man, wife and three children will now get £1.18s.6d a week, a rise of 3s.6d.
4th	HMS Nelson strikes a magnetic mine laid by U-31 at the entrance to Loch Ewe on the Scottish coast. Nelson is moved to Portsmouth for repairs where it remains until August 1940.
4th	The German submarine U-36 is torpedoed and sunk, with the loss of all hands, by the British submarine HMS Salmon off Stavanger. It is the first enemy submarine lost to a British one during the War.
9th	Corporal Thomas Priday becomes the first soldier of the British Expeditionary Force to be killed when he triggers a French land mine.
12th	The destroyer HMS Duchess (H64) sinks after a collision with the battleship HMS Barham (04) off the Mull of Kintyre in heavy fog. 124 men are lost.

The pocket battleship Graf Spee after being scuttled off Montevideo on the 17th December.

17th December: The Battle of the River Plate takes place between HMS Exeter, HMS Ajax, HMNZS Achilles and the German cruiser Admiral Graf Spee. The three Royal Navy cruisers found and engaged the Graf Spee off the estuary of the River Plate close to the coast of Uruguay in South America. In the ensuing battle, Exeter was severely damaged and forced to retire; Ajax and Achilles suffered moderate damage. The damage to Admiral Graf Spee, although not extensive, was critical; her fuel system was crippled. Ajax and Achilles shadowed the German ship until she entered the port of Montevideo to effect urgent repairs. After Graf Spee's captain Hans Langsdorff was told that his stay could not be extended beyond 72 hours, he scuttled his damaged ship rather than face the overwhelmingly superior force that the British had led him to believe was awaiting his departure.

18th	RAF Bomber Command, on a daylight mission to attack Kriegsmarine ships in the Battle of the Heligoland Bight, is repulsed by Luftwaffe fighter aircraft. This is the first 'named' air battle of the Second World War.

BRITISH PUBLICATIONS FIRST PRINTED IN 1939

- H. E. Bates' short story collection My Uncle Silas.
- Joyce Carey's novel Mister Johnson.
- James Hadley Chase's thriller No Orchids For Miss Blandish.
- Agatha Christie's novels Murder Is Easy and Ten Little Indians.
- Henry Green's novel Party Going.
- Aldous Huxley's novel After Many A Summer.
- Richard Llewellyn's novel How Green Was My Valley.
- Jan Struther's short story collection Mrs. Miniver.

NOTABLE BRITISH DEATHS

9th Jan	Sir Edwin Wood Thorp Farley, MBE (b. 1864) - Mayor of Dover, Kent from 1913 to 1919. Farley went to sea when he was twelve years old and sailed to India and China many times. He served on Dover Town Council for 27 years. For his services to Dover during the First World War he was appointed Member of the Order of the British Empire (MBE) in 1918 and knighted in the 1920 New Year Honours.
2nd Mar	Howard Carter (b. 9th May 1874) - Archaeologist and Egyptologist who became world-famous after discovering the intact tomb (designated KV62) of the 18th Dynasty Pharaoh, Tutankhamun (colloquially known as 'King Tut' and 'the boy king'), in November 1922.
6th Mar	Dorothea Frances Matilda 'Dora' Pertz. FLS (b. 14th March 1859) - Botanist who co-authored five papers with Francis Darwin, Charles Darwin's son. She was made a Fellow of the Linnean Society in 1905 and was among the first women admitted to full membership.

9th May - Lady Mary Heath (b. 10th November 1896) - Irish aviator and athlete who began life as Sophie Catherine Theresa Mary Peirce-Evans in Knockaderry, County Limerick. She was one of the founders of the Women's Amateur Athletic Association and was Britain's first women's javelin champion (she also set a disputed world record for the high jump). In 1926 Lady Heath became the first woman to hold a commercial flying licence in Britain. She also set records for altitude in a small plane and later a Shorts seaplane, and became the first woman to parachute from an aeroplane (landing in the middle of a football match). After her stunning solo flight from Cape Town to London in 1928 she went on to take a mechanic's qualification in the USA, another first for a woman.

25th Jun	Richard John Beattie Seaman (b. 4th February 1913) - One of the greatest pre-WW2 British Grand Prix drivers, commonly known as Dick Seaman. He famously drove for the Mercedes-Benz team from 1937-1939 in the Mercedes-Benz W154 car, winning the 1938 German Grand Prix. He died of his injuries after his car crashed into a tree and caught fire during lap 22 of the 1939 Belgian Grand Prix.
26th Jun	Ford Madox Ford (b. Ford Hermann Hueffer; 17th December 1873) - English novelist, poet, critic and editor whose journals, The English Review and The Transatlantic Review, were instrumental in the development of early 20th century English literature. Ford is now remembered for his novels The Good Soldier (1915), the Parade's End tetralogy (1924-28) and The Fifth Queen trilogy (1906-08).
6th Sep	Arthur Rackham (b. 19th September 1867) - Book illustrator who is widely regarded as one of the leading illustrators from the 'Golden Age' (1890-1918) of British book illustration.
3rd Dec	Princess Louise, Duchess of Argyll, VA, CI, GCVO, GBE, RRC, GCStJ (b. Louise Caroline Alberta; 18th March 1848) - The sixth child and fourth daughter of Queen Victoria and Prince Albert.

25 WORLDWIDE NEWS & EVENTS

1. 1st January - The Hewlett-Packard Company is founded in a one-car garage in Palo Alto by William Redington Hewlett and David Packard, and initially produced a line of electronic test equipment (HP has since become a multi-billion dollar company and was the world's leading PC manufacturer from 2007 to Q2 2013).

2. 5th January - Amelia Earhart, the American aviator and the 1st woman to fly solo across the Atlantic, is officially declared dead at 41 after her disappearance over the Pacific Ocean in 1937.

3. 13th January - Black Friday: 71 people die across Victoria in one of Australia's worst ever bushfires. Almost 20,000km² (4,942,000 acres, 2,000,000ha) of land is burned and several towns are entirely destroyed, including over 1,300 homes and 69 sawmills. The Royal Commission that resulted from the fire led to major changes in forest management.

4. 24th January - South central Chile is hit with an 8.3 magnitude earthquake at 11:33pm. The epicenter was the city of Chillan and it is estimated that around 30,000 people perished as a result of what was deadliest earthquake in Chile's history.

5. 10th February - Pope Pius XI (b. Ambrogio Damiano Achille Ratti; 31st May 1857), who was the head of the Catholic Church from the 6th February 1922, dies after failing health aged 81. He was the first sovereign of Vatican City, from its creation as an independent state on the 11th February 1929.

6. 28th March - Francisco Franco conquers Madrid with the help of pro-Franco forces inside the city. The following day, Valencia, which had held out under the guns of the Nationalists for close to two years, also surrendered. Victory was proclaimed on the 1st April when the last of the Republican forces surrendered, thus ending the Spanish Civil War.

7. 4th April - Faisal II becomes King of Iraq at age 3 following the death of his father, Ghazi, in a mysterious car incident. Faisal II reigned until 1958 when he was executed with numerous members of his family during the 14th July Revolution.

8. 9th April - African-American singer Marian Anderson performs before 75,000 people at the Lincoln Memorial in Washington, D.C. after having been denied the use of both the Constitution Hall, by the Daughters of the American Revolution (DAR), and of a public high school, by the federally controlled District of Columbia. First Lady Eleanor Roosevelt later resigned from the DAR because of their decision.

9. 30th April - Nylon fabric is first introduced to the general public at the New York World's Fair (Nylon stockings would go on sale for the first time in Wilmington, Delaware just six months later, on the 24th October).

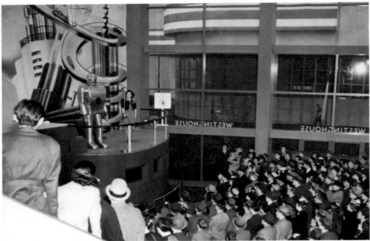

10. The World's Fair (30th April 1939 - 31st October 1940): Elektro, the 'moto-man' built by Westinghouse Electric Corp., performs marvels on stage for fairgoers: the 7-foot-tall robot could walk, talk, count on his fingers and even smoke a cigarette. He could say 700 words using a record player and could tell the difference between green and red.

11. May - Batman, created by Bob Kane and Bill Finger, makes his first appearance in Detective comics No.27. Later that Summer, Superman (who began as one of several anthology features in the National Periodical Publications comic book, Action Comics No.1, in June 1938) is launched into his own self-titled comic book, the first for any superhero.

12. | 20th May - Pan American Airways begins a trans-Atlantic mail service with the inaugural flight of its Boeing 314 flying boat Yankee Clipper from Port Washington, New York to Marseille.

13. | 4th June - The St. Louis, a ship carrying a cargo of 907 Jewish refugees, is denied permission to land in Florida after already having been turned away from Cuba. Forced to return to Europe, 254 of its passengers would later die in Nazi death camps during The Holocaust.

14. | 17th June - German criminal Eugen Weidmann (b. 5th February 1908) is executed by guillotine in France, the last public execution in that country. Executions by guillotine did though continue in private until the 10th September 1977 with the execution of Hamida Djandoubi.

15. 1st July - The starting gate, a machine used in the sports of thoroughbred horse and dog racing to ensure a fair start in a race, was used for the first time at Lansdowne Park in Vancouver, British Columbia, Canada. Invented by Clay Puett of Chillicothe, Texas, the U.S. patent was filed on the 7th August 1939 and issued to him on the 18th February 1941.

16. 15th July - Swiss psychiatrist and eugenicist Paul Eugen Bleuler (b. 30th April 1857), most notable for his contributions to the understanding of mental illness, dies. He coined many psychiatric terms, such as schizophrenia, schizoid, autism, depth psychology and ambivalence.

17. 2nd August - A letter written by Leó Szilárd and Albert Einstein is signed advising President of the United States, Franklin D. Roosevelt, of the potential use of uranium to construct an atomic bomb. It was delivered on the 11th October.

18. 27th August - Captain Erich Warsitz makes the first entirely turbojet powered flight in a Heinkel He 178.

19. 1st September - Robert Oppenheimer and Hartland Snyder publish a paper 'On Continued Gravitational Attraction', jointly predicting the existence of what will come to be called black holes. Oppenheimer is probably best remembered as the wartime head of the Los Alamos Laboratory and for his role in the Manhattan Project, the World War II undertaking that developed the first nuclear weapons used in the atomic bombings of Hiroshima and Nagasaki.

20. 5th September - World War II: The United States declares its neutrality in the war.

21. 23rd September - Austrian neurologist Sigmund Freud (b. Sigismund Schlomo Freud; 6th May 1856) dies. Freud was the founder of psychoanalysis, a clinical method for treating psychopathology through dialogue between a patient and a psychoanalyst.

22. 1st & 2nd November - Physicist Hans Ferdinand Mayer writes the Oslo Report on German weapons systems and passes it to the British Secret Intelligence Service. Describing current and future weapons systems, it was one of the most spectacular leaks in the history of military intelligence.

23. 16th November - Al Capone is paroled by the Federal Correctional Institution at Terminal Island in California (he had been transferred there after completing his sentence in Alcatraz some 10 months earlier). Capone was not well at this time and was suffering deteriorating mental health problems caused by late stage syphilis.

24. 28th November - James Naismith (b. 6th November 1861) dies. Naismith was a Canadian-American physical educator, physician, chaplain, sports coach and innovator, who invented the game of basketball aged 30 in 1891.

25. 15th December - The film Gone with the Wind, starring Vivien Leigh, Clark Gable, Olivia de Havilland and Leslie Howard, premieres at Loew's Grand Theatre in Atlanta, Georgia. It is based on Margaret Mitchell's best-selling novel and, at nearly four hours in length, is the longest American film made up to that date.

U.K. PERSONALITIES

BORN IN 1939

Brian William Luckhurst
5th February 1939 -
1st March 2005

Cricketer who played his entire county career (1958-1976) for Kent County Cricket Club. In total he played 355 matches for Kent, and also represented England in twenty one Test matches and three one day internationals. Over his career Luckhurst totalled 22,303 runs in first-class cricket, scoring a 1,000 or more runs in a season 14 times. He scored 48 centuries, with his highest score of 215 coming against Derbyshire at Derby in 1973.

Peter Purves
10th February 1939

Television presenter and actor. Purves played Steven Taylor in Doctor Who during the era of the First Doctor and later became a presenter on the BBC children's programme Blue Peter for eleven years. He has continued to make regular appearances on television, including an association with television coverage of the Crufts dog show. Purves is a noted pantomime director, enjoying a good working relationship with the Chuckle Brothers, and has directed over 30 pantomime productions.

Sir David Paradine Frost, OBE
7th April 1939 -
31st August 2013

Television host, media personality, journalist, comedian and writer who rose to prominence when he was chosen to host, That Was The Week That Was, in 1962. His success led to work on U.S. television and he became known for his television interviews with senior political figures, including the former U.S. President Richard Nixon. Frost has hosted a number of programmes most notably, Through The Keyhole (1987-2008), the Sunday morning programme Breakfast With Frost' (1993-2005), and Frost Over The World (2006-2012).

Reginald Leonard Smith, MBE
15th April 1939

Singer and songwriter who was among the first generation of British pop stars to emulate American rock and roll and is better known by his stage name Marty Wilde. From mid-1958 to the end of 1959, Wilde was one of the leading British rock and roll singers, along with Tommy Steele and Cliff Richard. He appeared regularly on the BBC Television show Six-Five Special and was the main regular artiste on ITV's popular Saturday music shows Oh Boy! and Boy Meets Girls.

Mary Isobel Catherine Bernadette O'Brien, OBE
16th April 1939 -
2nd March 1999

Pop singer and record producer who was professionally known as Dusty Springfield. At the peak of her career she was one of the most successful British female performers. She had sixteen top 20 hits on the U.K. Singles Chart and 6 on the U.S. Billboard Hot 100 between 1963 and 1989. Her image, supported by a peroxide blonde bouffant hairstyle, evening gowns, and heavy make-up, as well as her flamboyant performances made her an icon of the Swinging Sixties.

Alexander James 'Alex' Murphy, OBE
22nd April 1939

Former professional rugby league footballer and coach known as 'Murphy the Mouth' (or 'Yapper' by some referees). He represented Great Britain in 27 Tests and is regarded as one of the greatest half backs in the history of the British game. His club career was played at three clubs, St. Helens, Leigh and Warrington, and he became the first player to captain three different clubs to victory in the Challenge Cup Final. Murphy later returned to both Warrington and Leigh respectively as a football manager.

Sir Ian Murray McKellen, CH, CBE
25th May 1939

Actor whose career spans genres ranging from Shakespearean and modern theatre to popular fantasy and science fiction. He is the recipient of six Laurence Olivier Awards, a Tony Award, a Golden Globe Award, a Screen Actors Guild Award, a BIF Award, two Saturn Awards, four Drama Desk Awards, and two Critics' Choice Awards. He has also received two Oscar nominations, four BAFTA nominations and five Emmy Award nominations. A recipient of every major theatrical award in the UK, McKellen is regarded as a British cultural icon.

Terence Hardy 'Terry' Waite, CBE
31st May 1939

Humanitarian and author. As an envoy for the Church of England, he travelled to Lebanon in 1987 to try to secure the release of four hostages, including the journalist John McCarthy. He was himself kidnapped and held captive for 1,763 days (most of which was spent in solitary confinement) until he was eventually released on the 18th November 1991. Following his release he wrote his first book, Taken On Trust, an account of his captivity in Lebanon. It became a best-seller in the UK and internationally.

Dame Margaret Drabble, Lady Holroyd, DBE, FRSL
5th June 1939

Novelist, biographer and critic, who as of 2016 has published some 19 novels. Her third novel, The Millstone, brought her the John Llewellyn Rhys Memorial Prize in 1966, and her fourth, Jerusalem The Golden, won the James Tait Black Memorial Prize in 1967. Drabble was appointed Dame Commander of the Order of the British Empire (DBE) in the 2008 Birthday Honours. In 2003 she was the recipient of the St. Louis Literary Award and in 2011 she was awarded the Golden PEN Award for 'a Lifetime's Distinguished Service to Literature'.

Rachael Heyhoe Flint, Baroness Heyhoe Flint, OBE, DL
11th June 1939 -
18th January 2017

Cricketer, businesswoman and philanthropist. She was best known for being captain of England from 1966 to 1978, and was unbeaten in six Test series: in total, she played for the English women's cricket team from 1960 to 1982. Heyhoe Flint was captain when her team won the inaugural 1973 Women's Cricket World Cup, was also the first female cricketer to hit a six in a Test match and one of the first ten women to become a member of the Marylebone Cricket Club (MCC).

Sir John Young 'Jackie' Stewart, OBE
11th June 1939

Former Formula One racing driver nicknamed the 'Flying Scot'. Stewart competed in Formula One between 1965 and 1973, winning three World Drivers' Championships and twice finishing as runner-up. Outside of Formula One he narrowly missed out on a win at his first attempt at the Indianapolis 500 in 1966, and competed in the Can-Am series in 1971 and 1972. Stewart has been instrumental in improving the safety of motor racing, campaigning for better medical facilities and track improvements at motor racing circuits.

Dame Mary Elizabeth Peters, CH, DBE
6th July 1939

Former athlete who is best known for competing in the pentathlon and shot put. Peters won Britain's only athletics gold medal at the 1972 Munich Olympics. She narrowly beat the local favourite, West Germany's Heide Rosendahl, by 10 points in the pentathlon and set a world record score. In 1972 she also won the BBC Sports Personality of the Year award. Peters established a charitable Sports Trust (now known as the Mary Peters Trust) in 1975 to support talented young sportsmen and women from across Northern Ireland.

John Robert Parker Ravenscroft, OBE
30th August 1939 -
25th October 2004

Disc jockey, radio presenter, record producer and journalist known professionally as John Peel. He was the longest serving of the original BBC Radio 1 DJ's, broadcasting regularly from 1967 until his death in 2004. Peel's Radio 1 shows were notable for the regular 'Peel Sessions', which usually consisted of four songs recorded by an artist live in the BBC's studios, and which often provided the first major national coverage to bands that would later achieve great fame.

Eric 'Ricky' Tomlinson
26th September 1939

An actor, comedian, author, political activist and a qualified plasterer by trade. He is best known for his roles as Bobby Grant in Brookside, DCI Charlie Wise in Cracker, and Jim Royle in The Royle Family. He has also starred in several films, most notably, Mike Bassett: England Manager, Raining Stones and Hillsborough, a made-for-TV film about the families of the victims of the Hillsborough disaster. In October 2014 Tomlinson was awarded the Freedom of the City of Liverpool.

Hywel Rhodri Morgan
29th September 1939 -
17th May 2017

A Labour politician who was the First Minister of Wales and the Leader of Welsh Labour from 2000 to 2009. He was also the Assembly Member for Cardiff West from 1999 to 2011 and the Member of Parliament for Cardiff West from 1987 to 2001. Morgan was elected Chancellor of Swansea University on the 24th October 2011 and, as of 2017, is the longest-serving First Minister of Wales. His funeral in 2017 was the first Welsh national funeral, akin to a state funeral, as well being the first national funeral led by a humanist celebrant.

James Curran 'Jim' Baxter
29th September 1939 - 14th April 2001

Scottish professional footballer who is generally regarded as one of his country's greatest ever players. He was born, educated, and started his career in Fife. His peak playing years were in the early 1960's with the Glasgow club Rangers. At Rangers he helped them to win ten trophies between 1960 and 1965, and he became known to fans as 'Slim Jim'. From 1960 to 1967 he was a leading member of a strong Scottish international team, playing 34 times and scoring 3 goals.

George Reginald Cohen, MBE
22nd October 1939

Former professional footballer and the right-sided full back for the England side that won the 1966 World Cup. Cohen spent his entire 13 year playing career at Fulham after joining them in 1956. He played 37 times for England between 1964 and 1967, including winning 4-2 in the World Cup Final against West Germany, a match in which Cohen won his 30th cap as vice-captain of the team. Cohen has been inducted into the English Football Hall of Fame and is the uncle of rugby union World Cup winner Ben Cohen.

John Marwood Cleese
27th October 1939

Actor, voice actor, comedian, screenwriter and producer. He achieved success at the Edinburgh Festival Fringe and as a scriptwriter and performer on The Frost Report. In the late 1960's he co-founded Monty Python and in the mid-1970s, co-wrote and starred in the sitcom Fawlty Towers, with Cleese receiving the 1980 BAFTA for Best Entertainment Performance. Cleese has starred in a number of films including A Fish Called Wanda, Clockwise, two James Bond films as R and Q, two Harry Potter films, and the last three Shrek films.

Sylvia Ann Ibbetson
(née Butterfield), MBE
8th November 1939 - 25th September 2017

Actress known professionally as Liz Dawn and for her role as Vera Duckworth in the long-running British soap opera Coronation Street. She first started on the serial in 1974 and had a recurring role as a factory worker until her husband Jack, (played by Bill Tarmey) first appeared in 1979. She played the character of Vera for 34 years. For her role in the soap she received the Lifetime Achievement Award at the 2008 British Soap Awards. She was appointed an MBE in the 2000 Queens Birthday Honours.

POPULAR MUSIC

Judy Garland	No.1	Over The Rainbow
Glenn Miller & His Orchestra	No.2	Moonlight Serenade
The Andrews Sisters	No.3	Beer Barrel Polka (Roll Out The Barrel)
Vera Lynn	No.4	We'll Meet Again
Gracie Fields	No.5	Wish Me Luck As You Wave Me Goodbye
Bert Ambrose & His Orchestra	No.6	Nasty Uncle Adolf
Vera Lynn	No.7	I'm Sending A Letter To Santa Claus
Chick Henderson	No.8	Begin The Beguine
Billy Cotton & His Band	No.9	Washing On The Siegfried Line
The Ink Spots	No.10	If I Didn't Care

Note: During this era music was dominated by a number of 'Big Bands' and songs could be attributed to the band leader, the band name, the lead singer or a combination of these. On top of this the success of a song was tied to the sales of sheet music, so a popular song would often be perfomed by many different combinations of singers and bands and the contemporary charts would list the song, without clarifying whose version was the major hit. With this in mind it should be noted that although the above chart has been compiled with best intent it remains subjective.

Judy Garland
Over The Rainbow

Label:	Written by:	Length:
Brunswick	Harburg / Arlen	2 mins 49 secs

Judy Garland (b. Frances Ethel Gumm; 10th June 1922 - d. 22nd June 1969) was a singer, actress and vaudevillian. She was renowned for her contralto vocals and attained international stardom that continued throughout a career spanning more than 40 years. Over The Rainbow was written for the movie The Wizard of Oz and was sung by Garland in her starring role as Dorothy Gale. It won the Academy Award for Best Original Song and became Garland's signature song, and one of the most enduring standards of the 20th century.

Glenn Miller & His Orchestra
Moonlight Serenade

Label:	Written by:	Length:
Regal Zonophone	Glenn Miller	3 mins 22 secs

Alton Glenn Miller (b. 1st March 1904 - MIA 15th December 1944) was a big-band musician, arranger, composer and bandleader in the swing era. He was the best-selling recording artist from 1939 to 1943, leading one of the best-known big bands and scoring 23 No.1 hits. Moonlight Serenade, composed by Miller with subsequent lyrics by Mitchell Parish, was an immediate phenomenon when released in May 1939 as an instrumental arrangement. In 1991 Moonlight Serenade was inducted into the Grammy Hall of Fame.

The Andrews Sisters
Beer Barrel Polka (Roll Out The Barrel)

Label:	Written by:	Length:
Decca	Vejvoda / Brown / Timm	2 mins 50 secs

The Andrews Sisters were a close harmony singing group from the eras of swing and boogie-woogie. The group consisted of three sisters: LaVerne Sophia (b. 6th July 1911 - d. 8th May 1967), Maxene Angelyn (b. 3rd January 1916 - d. 21st October 1995) and Patricia Marie (b. 16th February 1918 - d. 30th January 2013). Throughout their long career the sisters sold well over 75 million records.

Vera Lynn
We'll Meet Again

Label:	Written by:	Length:
Decca	Ross Parker / Hughie Charles	3 mins 26 secs

Dame Vera Margaret Lynn, CH DBE OStJ (née Welch; b. 20th March 1917), widely known as 'the Forces' Sweetheart', is a singer, songwriter and actress, whose musical recordings and performances were enormously popular during the Second World War. During the war she toured Egypt, India and Burma as part of ENSA, giving outdoor concerts for the troops. We'll Meet Again is one of her most famous songs and resonated with soldiers, their families and sweethearts. The song also later gave its name to the 1943 musical of the same name in which Dame Vera Lynn played the lead role.

Gracie Fields
Wish Me Luck As You Wave Me Goodbye

Label:	Written by:	Length:
Victor	Harry Parr Davies / Phil Park	3 mins 3 secs

Dame Gracie Fields, DBE (b. Grace Stansfield; 9th January 1898 - d. 27th September 1979) was an actress, singer, comedian and a star of both cinema and music hall. 'Wish Me Luck as You Wave Me Goodbye' appeared in Fields' 1939 film Shipyard Sally. Over the years it has been performed and recorded by many artists, including Vera Lynn, Elsie Carlisle, Chas & Dave, Cyril Grantham and Jack Hylton, but it is Fields' version which has set the standard.

Bert Ambrose & His Orchestra
Nasty Uncle Adolf

Label:	Written by:	Length:
Decca	(Unknown)	3 mins 7 secs

Benjamin Baruch Ambrose (b. 11th September 1896 - d. 11th June 1971) was known professionally as Ambrose or Bert Ambrose. He was an English bandleader and violinist who became the leader of the highly acclaimed British dance band Bert Ambrose & His Orchestra in the 1930s. The song 'Nasty Uncle Adolf' featured Jack Cooper as the vocalist.

7 Vera Lynn
I'm Sending A Letter To Santa Claus

Label:	Written by:	Length:
Decca	Rogers / Williams	3 mins 20 secs

I'm Sending A Letter To Santa Claus was recorded by a number of artists in 1939, including Arthur Askey and Gracie Fields, but it was this version that most resonated with the public. Dame Vera Lynn is still recording to this day and in 2017 released the album Vera Lynn 100. The album reached No.3 in the charts, making her the oldest recording artist in the world, and first centenarian, to have a charting album.

8 Chick Henderson
Begin The Beguine

Label:	Written by:	Length:
Regal Zonophone	Cole Porter	3 mins 31 secs

Chick Henderson (b. 22nd November 1912 - d. 24th June 1944) was a singer who achieved popularity and acclaim as a prolific recording artist and performer of the British dance band era. Henderson made over 250 recordings throughout his career but it was in July 1939 when he recorded, with Joe Loss and his Orchestra, what would become his biggest-selling record, Begin The Beguine. It sold over a million copies and helped make household names of both the band and its singer.

⑨ Billy Cotton & His Band
Washing On The Siegfried Line

Label:	**Written by:**	**Length:**
Rex	Jimmy Kennedy	3 mins 22 secs

William Edward 'Billy' Cotton (b. 6th May 1899 - d. 25th March 1969) was a band leader and entertainer, and one of the few whose orchestras survived the British dance band era. 'Washing On The Siegfried Line' was written by Ulster songwriter Jimmy Kennedy whilst he was a Captain in the British Expeditionary Force during the early stages of WW2. The song was used as a morale-booster throughout the war.

---

⑩ The Ink Spots
If I Didn't Care

Label:	**Written by:**	**Length:**
Decca	Jack Lawrence	3 mins 4 secs

The Ink Spots, Bill Kenny (b. 12th June 1914 - d. 23rd March 1978), Deek Watson (b. 18th July 1909 - d. 4th November 1969), Charlie Fuqua (b. 20th October 1910 - d. 21st December 1971), and Hoppy Jones (b. 17th February 1905 - d. 18th October 1944), were a pop vocal group who gained international fame in the 1930s and 1940s. In 1989 the Ink Spots were inducted into the Rock and Roll Hall of Fame, and in 1999 they were inducted into the Vocal Group Hall of Fame. 'If I Didn't Care' became one of the best-selling singles of all time with over 19 million copies sold worldwide.

1939: TOP FILMS

1. **Gone With The Wind** - *MGM/Selznick*
2. **Mr. Smith Goes To Washington** - *Columbia*
3. **The Wizard Of Oz** - *MGM*
4. **Wuthering Heights** - *United Artists*
5. **Goodbye Mr. Chips** - *MGM*

OSCARS

Best Picture: Gone With The Wind

Best Director: Victor Fleming *(Gone With The Wind)*

Best Actor:	**Best Actress:**
Robert Donat *(Goodbye Mr. Chips)*	Vivien Leigh *(Gone With The Wind)*
Best Supporting Actor:	**Best Supporting Actress:**
Thomas Mitchell *(Stagecoach)*	Hattie McDaniel *(Gone With The Wind)*

GONE WITH THE WIND

Winner
of Ten
Academy
Awards

STARRING

CLARK GABLE
VIVIEN LEIGH
LESLIE HOWARD OLIVIA de HAVILLAND

Directed by: Victor Fleming - Runtime: 3 hours 58 minutes

This epic tale follows a woman's life during one of the most tumultuous periods in America's history. It follows her from her young, innocent days on a feudalistic plantation to the war-torn streets of Atlanta; from her first love whom she has always desired to three husbands; from the utmost luxury to absolute starvation and poverty; from her innocence to her understanding and comprehension of life.

STARRING

Clark Gable
Born: 1st February 1901
Died: 16th November 1960

Character:
Rhett Butler

Actor often referred to as 'The King of Hollywood'. Gable began his career as a stage actor and appeared as an extra in silent films between 1924 and 1926. He progressed to supporting roles for MGM in 1931 and landed his first leading role soon after. Gable was a leading man in more than 60 motion pictures over the following three decades, winning an Oscar for Best Actor in It Happened One Night (1934).

Vivien Leigh
Born: 5th November 1913
Died: 8th July 1967

Character:
Scarlett O'Hara

Stage and film actress, who completed her drama school education in 1935. She appeared in small roles at first, progressing to the role of heroine in Fire Over England (1937). During her 30 year career Leigh won two Academy Awards for Best Actress; for her performances in Gone with the Wind (1939) and A Streetcar Named Desire (1951). She also won a Tony Award for her work in the Broadway musical version of Tovarich (1963).

Thomas Mitchell
Born: 11th July 1892
Died: 17th December 1962

Character:
Gerald O'Hara

An actor who started his career on the stage in 1913, at one point touring with Charles Coburn's Shakespeare Company. Among Mitchells most famous roles throughout his long career are those of Gerald O'Hara in Gone With The Wind, Doc Boone in Stagecoach (1939), Uncle Billy in It's A Wonderful Life (1946) and Mayor Jonas Henderson in High Noon (1952). Mitchell was the first ever male actor to win an Oscar, an Emmy, and a Tony Award.

TRIVIA

Goofs	After Ashley Wilkes is carried into his room from a night at Belle's place, Melanie picks up a lamp with an electric cord attached (the film is set during the American Civil War and Reconstruction Era, 1861-1873). When Rhett kisses Scarlett goodbye right before he enlists, he drops his hat on the ground. He kisses her and picks it up from atop a fence post.
Interesting Facts	At nearly four hours long, this is the longest running of all motion pictures to win the prestigious Academy Award for Best Picture.

CONTINUED

Interesting Facts

The fact that Hattie McDaniel was unable to attend the premiere of the movie in racially segregated Atlanta outraged Clark Gable so much that he threatened to boycott it unless she could attend. He later relented when she convinced him to go.

When Gary Cooper turned down the part of Rhett Butler he was passionately against playing the role. He is quoted as saying 'Gone With The Wind is going to be the biggest flop in Hollywood history' and 'I'm just glad it'll be Clark Gable who's falling on his face and not Gary Cooper'.

Vivien Leigh later said that she hated kissing Clark Gable because of his bad breath, rumoured to be caused by his false teeth, a result of excessive smoking. According to Frank Buckingham, a technician who observed the film being made, Gable would sometimes eat garlic before his kissing scenes with Vivien Leigh.

The horse that Thomas Mitchell rode was later Silver in The Lone Ranger (1949).

Vivien Leigh worked for 125 days and received about $25,000. Clark Gable worked for 71 days and received over $120,000.

Gone With The Wind was nominated for 13 Academy Awards, of which it won 8.

For the premiere in Atlanta on the 15th December 1939 the governor declared a state holiday. Ticket prices for the showing were 40 times the usual going rate.

Quotes

Scarlett: Rhett, Rhett... Rhett, if you go, where shall I go? What shall I do?
Rhett Butler: Frankly, my dear, I don't give a damn.

Scarlett: Sir, you are no gentleman.
Rhett Butler: And you, Miss, are no lady.

MR. SMITH GOES TO WASHINGTON

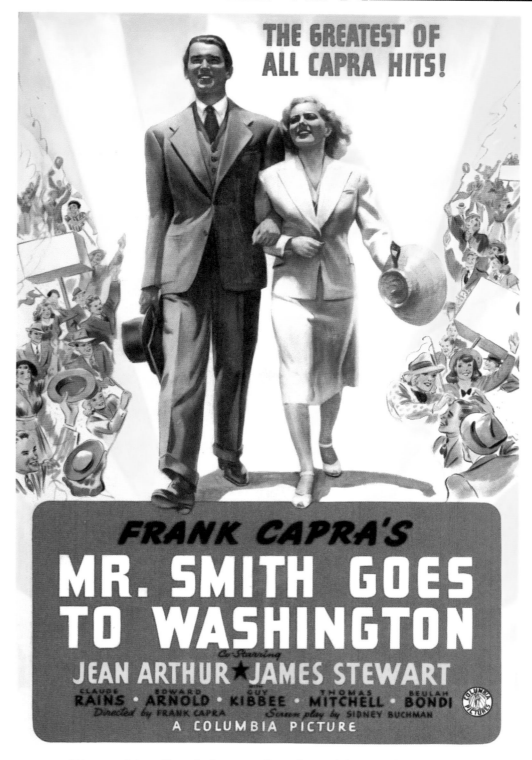

Directed by: Frank Capra - Runtime: 2 hours 9 minutes

A naive man is appointed to fill a vacancy in the United States Senate. His plans promptly collide with political corruption, but he doesn't back down.

STARRING

James Stewart
Born: 20th May 1908
Died: 2nd July 1997

Character:
Jefferson Smith

Actor and military officer who is among the most honoured and popular stars in film history. Stewart was known for his distinctive drawl and down-to-earth persona, which helped him often portray middle-class men struggling in crisis. Many of his films have become enduring classics. Stewart was nominated for five Academy Awards, winning one in competition for The Philadelphia Story (1940), and received an Academy Lifetime Achievement award in 1985.

Jean Arthur
Born: 17th October 1900
Died: 19th June 1991

Character:
Clarissa Saunders

Actress and a major film star of the 1930s and 1940s, born Gladys Georgianna Greene. She was discovered by Fox Film Studios whilst doing commercial modelling in New York City in the early 1920s and landed a one-year contract, debuting in the silent film Cameo Kirby (1923). Arthur was nominated for an Academy Award for Best Actress for her performance in The More the Merrier (1943) and has been called 'the quintessential comedic leading lady'.

Claude Rains
Born: 10th November 1889
Died: 30th May 1967

Character:
Senator Joseph Paine

Film and stage actor whose career spanned 46 years. After his debut as Dr. Jack Griffin in The Invisible Man (1933) he appeared in classic films such as The Adventures Of Robin Hood (1938), Mr. Smith Goes To Washington, Casablanca (1942), and Lawrence Of Arabia (1962). He was a Tony Award winning actor and was a four-time nominee for the Best Supporting Actor Academy Award. Rains was considered to be 'one of the screen's great character stars'.

TRIVIA

Goofs When Smith arrives in Washington on the train, he's seen walking towards the exit with a porter behind him carrying his bags. The next shot shows the same porter coming into the station carrying someone else's bags.

Interesting Facts In 1942, when a ban on American films was imposed in German-occupied France, theatres chose Mr. Smith Goes To Washington as their last movie before the ban went into effect. One Paris theatre reportedly screened the film nonstop for 30 days prior to the ban.

CONTINUED

Interesting Facts

Because Jean Arthur's left side was considered her best side, the sets were constructed so that whenever she entered she would be photographed from that side.

This film is one of five times that Beulah Bondi portrayed James Stewart's mother. The others occasions were in the films, Of Human Hearts (1938), Vivacious Lady (1938), It's a Wonderful Life (1946), and once on his television series, The Jimmy Stewart Show (1971).

Frank Capra reportedly received many letters over the years from individuals who were inspired by this film to take up politics.

Mr. Smith Goes To Washington is ranked No.5 on the American Film Institute's 100 Most Inspiring Movies of All Time (2006), and No.26 on its Greatest Movie of All Time (2007).

Quotes

Jefferson Smith: You see, boys forget what their country means by just reading The Land of the Free in history books. When they get to be men they forget even more. Liberty's too precious a thing to be buried in books, Miss Saunders. Men should hold it up in front of them every single day of their lives and say: I'm free to think and to speak. My ancestors couldn't, I can, and my children will. Boys ought to grow up remembering that.

Jefferson Smith: What's your first name?
Clarissa Saunders: Why?
Jefferson Smith: Well, I, eh, everybody just calls you plain Saunders.
Clarissa Saunders: Well, I also answer to whistles.

Jefferson Smith: I wouldn't give you two cents for all your fancy rules if, behind them, they didn't have a little bit of plain, ordinary, everyday kindness and a little looking out for the other fella, too.

THE WIZARD OF OZ

Directed by: Victor Fleming - Runtime: 1 hour 42 minutes

Dorothy Gale is swept away by a tornado in Kansas to the magical land of Oz. She embarks on a quest to see the Wizard whom she hopes can help her return home, and also help her friends.

STARRING

Judy Garland
Born: 10th June 1922
Died: 22nd June 1969

Character:
Dorothy Gale

Singer and actress who began performing in vaudeville with her two older sisters and was signed to Metro-Goldwyn-Mayer as a teenager. Born Frances Ethel Gumm, she made more than two dozen films with MGM including nine with Mickey Rooney. Garland's most famous role was as Dorothy Gale in The Wizard of Oz. Aged 39 she became the youngest and first female recipient of the Cecil B. DeMille Award.

Frank Morgan
Born: 1st June 1890
Died: 18th September 1949

Characters:
Professor Marvel / The Wizard of Oz / The Gatekeeper / The Carriage Driver / The Guard

Character actor who is best known as a Metro-Goldwyn-Mayer contract player and as the titular character in The Wizard of Oz. He made his film debut in The Suspect (1916). His career expanded with the advent of talkies and by the mid-1930s MGM had signed him to a lifetime contract. Morgan was nominated for two Academy Awards during his career, one for Best Actor in The Affairs Of Cellini (1934) and one for Best Supporting Actor for Tortilla Flat (1942).

Ray Bolger
Born: 10th January 1904
Died: 15th January 1987

Character:
The Scarecrow

Actor, singer, and dancer (particularly of tap) of vaudeville, stage and screen. Bolger started his career in the silent film era and is best known for his portrayal of the Scarecrow in The Wizard of Oz. In the 1950s he hosted his own television show 'Where's Raymond' which ran for 2 seasons. For his contributions to the film industry Bolger received a motion pictures star on the Hollywood Walk of Fame in 1960.

TRIVIA

Goofs | When the wicked witch sends out the flying monkeys, she says, 'And send the little insects on out ahead to take the fight out of them'. Those 'insects' are Jitterbugs. The Jitterbug scene was filmed but later cut; the line however was not removed.

At the end of the 'Merry Old Land of Oz' song the characters are all laughing but all their mouths are still singing.

When Dorothy uses the knocker on the door to the Emerald City, four knocks are heard although she only hits the door three times. The first is heard as she is drawing the knocker back.

CONTINUED

Interesting Facts

Margaret Hamilton, a lifelong fan of the 'Oz' books, was ecstatic when she learned the producers were considering her for a part in the film. When she phoned her agent to find out what role she was up for, her agent simply replied, 'The witch, who else?'

The Scarecrow face makeup that Ray Bolger wore consisted, in part, of a rubber prosthetic with a woven pattern to suggest burlap cloth. By the time the film was finished the prosthetic had left a pattern of lines on his face that took more than a year to vanish.

The horses in Emerald City palace were coloured with Jell-O crystals. The relevant scenes had to be shot quickly, before the horses started to lick it off.

When the wardrobe department was looking for a coat for Frank Morgan (Prof. Marvel / The Wizard), it decided it wanted one that looked like it had once been elegant but had since 'gone to seed'. They visited a second-hand store and purchased an entire rack of coats, from which Morgan, the head of the wardrobe department and director Victor Fleming chose one they felt gave off the perfect appearance of shabby gentility. One day, while he was on set in the coat, Morgan idly turned out one of the pockets and discovered a label indicating that the coat had been made for L. Frank Baum. Mary Mayer, a unit publicist for the film, contacted the tailor and Baum's widow, who both verified that the coat had once been owned by the author of the original 'Wizard of Oz' books. After the filming was completed, the coat was presented to Mrs. Baum.

Quotes

Scarecrow: I haven't got a brain... only straw.
Dorothy: How can you talk, if you haven't got a brain?
Scarecrow: I don't know, but some people without brains do an awful lot of talking don't they?
Dorothy: Yes. I guess you're right.

Wicked Witch of the West: Just try and stay out of my way. Just try! I'll get you my pretty, and your little dog too!

Auntie Em Gale: Almira Gulch, just because you own half the county doesn't mean that you have the power to run the rest of us. For 23 years, I've been dying to tell you what I thought of you! And now... well, being a Christian woman, I can't say it!

WUTHERING HEIGHTS

I am torn with *Desire*...tortured by hate!

SAMUEL GOLDWYN
presents

WUTHERING HEIGHTS

co-starring

MERLE OBERON · LAURENCE OLIVIER · DAVID NIVEN

with FLORA ROBSON · DONALD CRISP · GERALDINE FITZGERALD · *Released thru* UNITED ARTISTS
Directed by WILLIAM WYLER

Directed by: William Wyler - Runtime: 1 hour 44 minutes

A servant from the remote moorland farmhouse of Wuthering Heights tells a traveller the unfortunate tale of lovers Cathy and Heathcliff.

STARRING

Merle Oberon
Born: 19th February 1911
Died: 23rd November 1979

Character:
Cathy

An Anglo-Indian actress who began her film career in British films as Anne Boleyn in The Private Life of Henry VIII (1933). After her success in The Scarlet Pimpernel (1934) she travelled to the United States to make films for Samuel Goldwyn. She was nominated for an Academy Award for Best Actress for her performance in The Dark Angel (1935) but her most renowned performance was in Wuthering Heights.

Laurence Olivier
Born: 22nd May 1907
Died: 11th July 1989

Character:
Heathcliff

Actor and director who dominated the British stage of the mid-20th century. He also worked in films throughout his career playing more than fifty cinema roles. For his on-screen work he received four Academy Awards, two British Academy Film Awards, five Emmy Awards and three Golden Globe Awards. He is also commemorated in the Laurence Olivier Awards, given annually by the Society of London Theatre.

David Niven
Born: 1st March 1910
Died: 29th July 1983

Character:
Edgar

An actor and novelist who first appeared as an extra in the film There Goes The Bride (1932), and went on to appear in nearly a hundred other films. He is probably best known for his roles as Squadron Leader Peter Carter in A Matter Of Life And Death (1946), Phileas Fogg in Around The World In 80 Days (1956) and as Sir Charles Lytton in The Pink Panther (1963). Niven won the Academy Award for Best Actor for his performance in Separate Tables (1958).

TRIVIA

Goofs	When Cathy returns to Wuthering Heights to confront Heathcliff about his engagement to Isabella, she turns to leave and when she opens the door to storm out you can see the set behind the door for a split second.
	As Cathy walks uphill to see Heathcliff her entire costume changes.
Interesting Facts	The film only depicts sixteen of the novel's thirty-four chapters and is set in 19th century instead of 1771-1801.

CONTINUED

Interesting Facts Laurence Olivier found himself becoming increasingly annoyed with William Wyler's exhausting style of film-making. After yet another take he is said to have exclaimed, 'For God's sake, I did it sitting down. I did it with a smile. I did it with a smirk. I did it scratching my ear. I did it with my back to the camera. How do you want me to do it?' Wyler's retort was, 'I want it better'. Later however Olivier said these multiple takes helped him succeed as a film actor.

Around 1,000 heather plants were imported from England and replanted at Thousand Oaks to help simulate the look of the moors. They enjoyed the Californian sunshine so much that they tripled in size and had to be cut back before filming began.

Quote **Cathy:** Heathcliff, make the world stop right here. Make everything stop and stand still and never move again. Make the moors never change and you and I never change.
Heathcliff: The moors and I will never change. Don't you, Cathy.
Cathy: I can't. I can't. No matter what I ever do or say, Heathcliff, this is me now; standing on this hill with you. This is me forever.

GOODBYE MR. CHIPS

"The Best Picture of Any Year"

Robert **DONAT**

GOODBYE MR. CHIPS

Goodbye Mr. Chips

WITH *Greer* **GARSON**

A SAM WOOD *Production*

SCREEN PLAY BY R. C. SHERRIFF, CLAUDINE WEST AND
ERIC MASCHWITZ · *Produced by* VICTOR SAVILLE

Directed by: Sam Wood - Runtime: 1 hour 54 minutes

An old classics teacher looks back over his long career remembering pupils and colleagues, and above all the idyllic courtship and marriage that transformed his life.

STARRING

Robert Donat
Born: 18th March 1905
Died: 9th June 1958

Character:
Charles Edward Chipping,
'Mr. Chips'

Film and stage actor who made his first stage appearance in 1921 at the age of 16 with Henry Baynton's company at the Prince of Wales Theatre, Birmingham. He is best remembered for his roles in Alfred Hitchcock's The 39 Steps (1935) and Goodbye, Mr. Chips (for which he won the Academy Award for Best Actor). Donat suffered from chronic asthma throughout his career which ultimately limited his film appearances to just twenty in total.

Greer Garson
Born: 29th September 1904
Died: 6th April 1996

Character:
Katherine Ellis

Actress, born Eileen Evelyn Greer Garson, whose popularity was at its peak during the Second World War. She was listed by the Motion Picture Herald as one of America's top-ten box office draws from 1942 to 1946. Garson received seven Academy Award nominations during her career, including a record five consecutive nominations. Her only win was taking the Academy Award for Best Actress in Mrs. Miniver (1942).

Terry Kilburn
Born: 25th November 1926

Characters:
John Colley / Peter Colley I
/ Peter Colley II / Peter
Colley III

Actor who was born in London and moved to Hollywood at the age of 10. He is best known for his roles as a child actor in the late 1930s and the early 1940s, appearing in films such as A Christmas Carol (1938) and Goodbye, Mr. Chips. Upon finishing high school Kilburn concentrated on stage work, making his Broadway debut in a 1952 revival of George Bernard Shaw's Candida. Afterwards Kilburn remained committed to live performances as both an actor and director.

TRIVIA

Interesting Facts

The poster art depicts a youthful Robert Donat (as he appears in the early scenes of the film) with the young Greer Garson. However the two never appear together like this in the film. Chips is about fifty years old when he first meets Katherine who is in her mid-twenties.

At the 12th Academy Awards Goodbye Mr. Chips was nominated in seven categories. Robert Donat was its only winner taking the Oscar for Best Actor by beating, Clark Gable in Gone With The Wind, James Stewart in Mr. Smith Goes To Washington, Mickey Rooney in Babes In Arms and Laurence Olivier in Wuthering Heights.

CONTINUED

Interesting Facts | 'Lux Radio Theatre' broadcast a radio adaptation of the film on the 20th November 1939 with Laurence Olivier as Mr. Chips.

The film takes place from 1870 to 1933.

34-year-old Robert Donat ages 63 years over the course of the film. He remarked: 'As soon as I put the moustache on, I felt the part, even if I did look like a geat airedale come out of a puddle'.

Greer Garson was initially offered a contract for MGM in 1937 but refused all the minor parts she was offered until she got the role of Kathy Ellis in this film.

Mr. Chips was modelled on W.H. Balgarnie, novelist James Hilton's old classics master who taught for over 50 years at The Leys public school in Cambridge.

Quotes | **Katherine:** It must be tremendously interesting to be a schoolmaster, to watch boys grow up and help them along; to see their characters develop and what they become when they leave school and the world gets hold of them. I don't see how you could ever get old in a world that's always young.

[dying words]
Mr. Chips: I thought I heard you saying it was a pity... pity I never had any children. But you're wrong. I have. Thousands of them. Thousands of them... and all boys.

Sporting Winners

Home Nations Rugby
Wales

Position	Nation	Played	Won	Draw	Lost	For	Against	+/-	Points
1	**Wales**	**3**	**2**	**0**	**1**	**18**	**6**	**+12**	**4**
2	Ireland	3	2	0	1	17	10	+7	4
3	England	3	2	0	1	12	11	+1	4
4	Scotland	3	0	0	3	12	32	-20	0

The 1939 Home Nations Championship was the thirty-fifth series of the rugby union Home Nations Championship. Including the previous incarnations as the Five Nations, and prior to that, the Home Nations, this was the fifty-second series of the northern hemisphere rugby union championship. Six matches were played between the 21st January and 18th March. It was contested by England, Ireland, Scotland and Wales.

Date	Team		Score		Team	Location
21/01/1939	England	+	3-0	🏴	Wales	London
04/02/1939	Wales	🏴	11-3	✕	Scotland	Cardiff
11/02/1939	England	+	0-5	🍀	Ireland	London
25/02/1939	Ireland	🍀	12-3	✕	Scotland	Dublin
11/03/1939	Ireland	🍀	0-7	🏴	Wales	Belfast
18/03/1939	Scotland	✕	6-9	+	England	Edinburgh

This was the last tournament that did not feature France, which had been expelled after the 1931 tournament over allegations of professionalism and administrative deficiencies. France was readmitted later in 1939 but the start of World War II in Europe in September put international rugby on hold; it would not resume again until 1947.

Calcutta Cup

Scotland ✕ 6-9 + England

The Calcutta Cup was first awarded in 1879 and is the rugby union trophy awarded to the winner of the match (currently played as part of the Six Nations Championship) between England and Scotland.

BRITISH GRAND PRIX - RAYMOND MAYS

Raymond Mays with his ERA at Brooklands in 1937.

The 1939 Campbell Trophy was a non-championship Grand Prix held at Brooklands, near Weybridge in Surrey, on the 7th August. The race was won by Raymond Mays - Mays also had the fastest lap with an average speed of 77.79mph.

Pos.	Country	Driver	Car
1	**United Kingdom**	**Raymond Mays**	**ERA D-Type**
2	Thailand	Prince Bira	Maserati 8CM
3	United Kingdom	Peter Aitken	ERA B-Type

The Brooklands motor racing circuit opened in 1907 and was the world's first purpose-built racing track. The 1939 Campbell Trophy was the last race ever to be held at Brooklands.

AIACR EUROPEAN CHAMPIONSHIP

Pos.	Country	Driver	Constructor	Race Wins	Points
1	**Germany**	**Hermann Paul Müller**	**Auto Union**	**1**	**12**
2	Germany	Hermann Lang	Mercedes-Benz	2	14
3	Germany	Rudolf Caracciola	Mercedes-Benz	1	17

The 1939 Grand Prix season was the seventh AIACR European Championship season. The championship winner was never officially announced by the AIACR due to the outbreak of World War II less than two weeks after the final event in Switzerland. At that time, it was also undecided which scoring system would be used, the old minimum points system that basically counted positions, or the French maximum points system similar to the modern one. Using the old minimum points system Müller was the winner, using the maximum points system Lang would have been the winner.

GRAND NATIONAL - WORKMAN

The 1939 Grand National was the 98th renewal of this world famous horse race and took place at Aintree Racecourse near Liverpool on the 24th March. Workman, trained by Jack Ruttle and ridden by Irish jockey Tim Hyde, won the race by three lengths.

Thirty-seven horses ran in the National competing for the £10,000 in prize money - all 37 horses returned safely to the stables.

	Name	Jockey	Age	Weight	Odds
1st	**Workman**	**Tim Hyde**	**9**	**10st 6lb**	**100/8**
2nd	MacMoffatt	Ian Alder	-	-	25/1
3rd	Kilstar	George Archibald	-	-	8/1
4th	Cooleen	Jack Fawcus	-	-	22/1
5th	Symaethis	Matthew Feakes	-	-	66/1

EPSOM DERBY - BLUE PETER

The Derby Stakes is Britain's richest horse race and the most prestigious of the country's five Classics. First run in 1780 this Group 1 flat horse race is open to three year old thoroughbred colts and fillies. The race takes place at Epsom Downs in Surrey over a distance of one mile, four furlongs and 10 yards (2,423 metres) and is scheduled for early June each year.

Photo: British-bred and trained thoroughbred racehorse Blue Peter (1936-1957) is seen being ridden home by Eph Smith to defeat Heliopolis by four lengths in the Derby. Blue Peter was bred and owned by the 6th Earl of Rosebery, and trained by Jack Jarvis.

FOOTBALL LEAGUE CHAMPIONS

England

Pos.	Team	F	A	Points
1	**Everton**	**88**	**52**	**59**
2	Wolverhampton Wanderers	88	39	55
3	Charlton Athletic	75	59	50
4	Middlesbrough	93	74	49
5	Arsenal	55	41	47

Scotland

Pos.	Team	F	A	Points
1	**Rangers**	**112**	**55**	**59**
2	Celtic	99	53	48
3	Aberdeen	91	61	46
4	Heart of Midlothian	98	70	45
5	Falkirk	73	63	45

FA CUP WINNERS - PORTSMOUTH

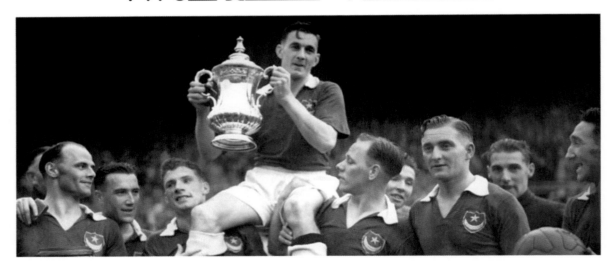

Portsmouth   **4-1**   **Wolverhampton Wanderers**

Barlow ⚽ 29'   Dorsett ⚽ 54'
Anderson ⚽ 43'
Parker ⚽ 46' ⚽ 71'

Referee: T. Thompson - Attendance: 99,370

The 1939 FA Cup Final took place on the 29th April at Wembley Stadium. As a result of the suspension of the FA Cup for the duration of the Second World War it would be 1946 before it was played again. (Photo: Portsmouth Captain Jimmy Guthrie being carried aloft by his team mates after winning the FA Cup).

GOLF - OPEN CHAMPIONSHIP - DICK BURTON

The 1939 Open Championship was the 74th to be played and was held between the 5th and 7th July over the Old Course at St Andrews, Fife, Scotland. Dick Burton won his only major title, two strokes ahead of runner-up Johnny Bulla, to take the Claret Jug and winner's prize money of £100. It was the last Open played for seven years due to World War II.

WORLD SNOOKER CHAMPIONSHIP - JOE DAVIS

Joe Davis ✠ 43 - 30 ✠ Sidney Smith

The 1939 World Snooker Championship was held at the Thurston's Hall in London between the 23rd January and 4th March. There were a record 15 entries for the Championship with the numbers in the competition proper increased from 8 to 12. Joe Davis won his 13th consecutive World title by defeating Sidney Smith in the final. Fred Davis made the highest break of the tournament with 113.

WIMBLEDON

Ladies Singles Champion - Alice Marble / Men's Singles Champion - Bobby Riggs

The 1939 Wimbledon Championships took place on the outdoor grass courts at the All England Lawn Tennis and Croquet Club in Wimbledon, London, and ran from the 26th June until the 7th July. It was the 59th staging of the Wimbledon Championships and the third Grand Slam tennis event of 1939. Due to World War II the tournament would not be held again until 1946.

Men's Singles Final:

Country	Player	Set 1	Set 2	Set 3	Set 4	Set 5
United States	Bobby Riggs	2	8	3	6	6
United States	Elwood Cooke	6	6	6	3	2

Women's Singles Final:

Country	Player	Set 1	Set 2
United States	Alice Marble	6	6
United Kingdom	Kay Stammers	2	0

Men's Doubles Final:

Country	Players	Set 1	Set 2	Set 3	Set 4
United States	Bobby Riggs / Elwood Cooke	6	3	6	9
United Kingdom	Charles Hare / Frank Wilde	3	6	3	7

Women's Doubles Final:

Country	Players	Set 1	Set 2
United States	Alice Marble / Sarah Fabyan	6	6
United States / United Kingdom	Helen Jacobs / Billie Yorke	1	0

Mixed Doubles Final:

Country	Players	Set 1	Set 2
United States	Bobby Riggs / Alice Marble	9	6
United Kingdom	Frank Wilde / Nina Brown	7	1

County Championship Cricket Winners - Yorkshire

1939 saw the 46th officially organised running of the County Championship. It was the last for six years due to World War II and was won by Yorkshire County Cricket Club, their 21st Championship. 1939 was the one and only season in which English cricket adopted the eight-ball over.

Pos.	Team	Played	Won	Lost	Drawn	Points	Average
1	**Yorkshire**	**28**	**20**	**4**	**0**	**260**	**9.28**
2	Middlesex	22	14	6	0	180	8.18
3	Gloucestershire	26	15	7	0	196	7.53
4	Essex	24	12	10	0	170	7.08
5	Kent	26	14	9	0	180	6.92

England Vs West Indies - Test Series

The West Indies cricket team toured England during the 1939 season and played a three-match Test series. England won the series 1-0 with two matches drawn. The tour was abandoned a few days after the third test match because of the worsening international situation with World War II imminent.

1st Test │ West Indies v England at Lord's, London - June 24th, 26th, 27th

Result │ England won by 8 wickets

Innings	Team	Score	Overs	Team	Score	Overs
1st Innings	West Indies	277	81.4	England	404/5d	95
2nd Innings	West Indies	225	69.4	England	100/2	17.7

2nd Test │ England v West Indies at Old Trafford, Manchester - July 22nd, 24th, 25th

Result │ Match Drawn

Innings	Team	Score	Overs	Team	Score	Overs
1st Innings	England	164/7d	55.2	West Indies	133	35.4
2nd Innings	England	128/6d	38	West Indies	43/4	15.6

3rd Test │ England v West Indies at The Oval, London - August 19th, 21st, 22nd

Result │ Match Drawn

Innings	Team	Score	Overs	Team	Score	Overs
1st Innings	England	352	73.3	West Indies	498	101.5
2nd Innings	England	366/3d	76	West Indies	-	-

THE COST OF LIVING

GINGER PUDDING WITH BIRD'S CUSTARD HOT

... there's nothing like

BIRD'S

CUSTARD & JELLIES

COMPARISON CHART

	1939 Price	1939 Price (Including inflation)	2018 Price	Real Term % Change
3 Bedroom House	£700	£44,778	£227,874	+408.9%
Weekly Income	£1.19s.5d	£126.07	£535	+324.4%
Pint Of Beer	8d	£2.13	£3.60	+69.0%
Cheese (lb)	1s.4d	£4.26	£3.38	-20.7%
Bacon (lb)	1s.8d	£5.33	£3.34	-37.3%
The Beano	2d	53p	£2.50	+371.7%

SHOPPING

Stork Margarine / Silver Seal Margarine (per lb)	8d
Jacobs Cream Crackers (½lb)	6½d
McDougall's Self-Raising Flour	1½d
Kraft Miracle Whip Salad Dressing (small jar)	6d
Maggi's Soups (3 platefuls)	2d
Rowntree's Kitkat Chocolate Crisp	2d
Fry's Chocolate Sandwich (2oz)	2d
Mars Bar	2d
Whiteways Non-Alcoholic Cydrax (bottle)	9d
Nipits Voice, Throat & Chest Pastilles (tin)	3d
Amami Hair Wave Set	6d
Newsheaf All Purpose Soap	4½d
Mcleans Peroxide Tooth Paste (giant tube)	1s.6d
Colgate Dental Cream	10½d
Kemdex Oxygen Denture Cleanser	1s
Alka-Seltzer	1s
Californian Poppy Beauty Treatment Box	2s.6d
Bu-To Odourless Depilatory	2s.6d
Snowfire Tablet For Chapped Hands	3d
Cutex Nail Polish (bottle)	9d
Trims Nail Polish Remover (3 months supply)	6d
Iron Jelloids (10 days supply)	1s.3d
Rennies (25)	6d
Yeast-Vite - The Lightning Pick-Me-Up (small bottle)	6d
Sunlight Flakes Washing Soap	6d
Paddy Washing Powder	3½d

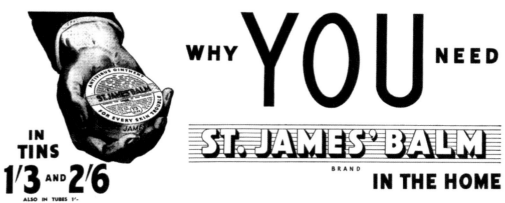

JACOB'S CREAM CRACKERS

"Thank you for telling me about Jacob's —they **are** the only biscuits with the real Cream Cracker flavour"

6½ᵈ per ½lb nett

Price not applicable to Eire

W. & R. Jacob & Co. (Liverpool) Ltd.

"Says she's fussy about food—but her Cooker's a disgrace!"

"If only she'd clean smoothly with VIM"

COLGATE
Dental Cream
Price Reduction

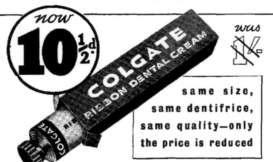

now **10½ᵈ**

was

COLGATE RIBBON DENTAL CREAM

same size, same dentifrice, same quality—only the price is reduced

the tremendous demand for Colgate's, the world's most popular toothpaste, has made possible this price reduction.

This was the largest shilling tube of toothpaste on the market. Now the *same* tube is to be sold at 10½d. More brilliant smiles, more mouth-freshness, more breath-fragrance

. . . everything Colgate's has always offered you is now yours for *less!* Change over to Colgate's now. Get more for your money—and brighter teeth into the bargain !

COLGATE RIBBON DENTAL CREAM
—biggest value . . . 10½ᵈ.

Apples for health

so-

Bulmer's for me!

Up from the country, fresh from the great orchard valleys of the West, comes Bulmer's Cider to bring health and vitality to people in town and city. These country people have a reputation for living long and living well, and its generations they've known what we townspeople are fast discovering— "Apples for Health." So order Bulmer's Cider when you are "stepping out." It is just the thing to make the party sparkle and to quench your thirst. You see, Bulmer's Cider is made from the purest apple juice and matured like wine in great oak vats.

BULMER'S IN SMALL BOTTLES IS OBTAINABLE AT HOTELS, RESTAURANTS, ROAD-HOUSES, ETC.

Bulmer's Cider, the great home favourite in the familiar bottles, is also obtainable in smaller bottles at all first-class Hotels, Road-Houses and Restaurants. When lunching or dining out remember your A.B.C. and order A Bulmer's Cider, the most delicious cider in the world.

Apples Bulmer's Cider

THE A·B·C OF HEALTH

H. P. BULMER & CO., LTD., HEREFORD. The Largest Cider Makers in the World.

CLOTHES

Women's Clothing

Samuel Soden Natural Grey Squirrel Fur Coat	12gns
Real Harris Tweed Coat	£2.15s
Derry & Toms Superfine Quality Fur Felt Hat	12s.9d
Swan & Edgar 3-Piece Suit	£4
Knitted Wool Jumper Suit	£1
Derry & Toms Satin Backed Ottoman Frock	£1.10s
C&A Swirl Print Dresses	9s.11d
Thomas Wallis All Wool Afgalaine Frock	7s.6d
Pontings Hand-Embroidered Blouse	5s
Pontings Flannel Skirts	5s
Swan & Edgar Floral Nightdress	8s
Floral Artificial Silk Slip & Knicker Set	6s
Cuban Leather Calf Tie Shoes	15s
Selfridges Brogue Shoes	5s
Pull-On Doeskin Gloves	2s.9d

The Gift of being well-groomed

BRYLCREEM

THE PERFECT HAIR DRESSING

TONIGHT they're dining at the Mayfair; then on to a theatre and dancing till the early hours. Tomorrow they're full up too —not an evening before Friday week. You see them everywhere, the man-about-town and his constant companion—Brylcreem. However long the night, Brylcreem keeps his hair immaculate. Christmas is a busy time for them both, and he can always do with an extra jar. The big bottle with the pump attachment makes an ideal gift.

In bottles and tubes 1⁄-

Larger bottles 1⁄6 1⁄9 2⁄6

Pumps to fit bottles . . . 2⁄-

At all Chemists and Hairdressers

County Perfumery Co. Ltd., North Circular Road, W. Twyford, N.W.10

Men's Clothing

Selfridges Mens Overcoat	£1.10s
Strong Made Fleecy Lined Weathercoat	8s.9d
Yorkshire Tweed 4-Piece Sports Suit	£2.15s
Gamage Made To Measure Suit	£2.9s.6d
Radiac Shirt With Multiple Weave Collars & Cuffs	7s.11d
Mens Smart Poplin Tennis Shirt	3s.6d
Genuine London Busmen's Trousers	5s.9d
Winter-Weight Woolen Dressing Gown	15s
Selfridges Winceyette Pyjamas	4s.6d
Medium Weight All-Wool Underwear	3s.11d
Naval Service Socks	1s
Gamage Service Boots	10s
Duraped Monk Style Shoes	8s.9d

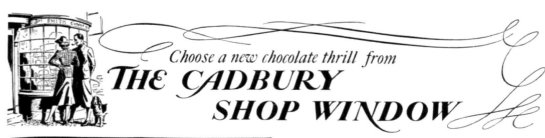

Choose a new chocolate thrill from

THE CADBURY SHOP WINDOW

¼ lb. MILK TURKISH DELIGHT FILLED BLOCK
4d
Another best seller in the Cadbury Filled Block Range

1 lb. CONTINENTAL
For the connoisseur of fine quality chocolates
5/-
Also in ½ lb. boxes at 2/6

1 lb. KING GEORGE V.
4/-
Cadburys most popular chocolates at the price

DAIRY MILK BLOCK
1d
Cadburys Dairy Milk is the most famous chocolate in the world. You get a generous block for a penny

MILK DROPS
4d
PER QTR.
A special favourite with the children. You get over 100 drops for 4d.

BOURNVILLE ROASTED ALMOND BLOCK
2d
Rich, crisp almonds blended with the finest plain chocolate

WRAPPED DAIRY MILK FLAKE
2d
Cadburys Dairy Milk Chocolate in its smoothest, milkiest form

MILK TRAY MARZIPAN DIAMONDS
6d PER QTR.
Sweet tooths will find these scrumptious

MILK WALNUT BLOCK
2d
Tasty, tangy walnuts sunk into Cadburys famous Milk Chocolate

½ lb. CARTON DAIRY MILK ASSORTED BISCUITS
7½d
A new thrill for the tea-table

½ lb. VOGUE
1/6
For a very particular gift—or any special treat to yourself

MILK BARS
½d
Remember how you used to gorge them? Your kiddies love them, too!

FLAT 20 MILK NEAPOLITANS
6d
Handy for the pocket—in size and price! (Also Plain)

WHIPPED CREME WALNUT
2d
The whole family eats milk whipped creme walnuts

DAIRY CARAMELS (MILK COVERED)
4d
PER QTR
U-u-m! Just taste how good they are!

1/6 BOX WAFER BISCUITS
The finest chocolate biscuit of them all! 12 in a box

MILK MARSHMALLOW
2d
If you like luxury, taste this. It's gorgeous!

MILK BRAZIL BLOCK
2d
Now—Brazil nuts and milk chocolate—a wonder feast for 2d!

¼ lb. MILK COFFEE & TRUFFLE FILLED BLOCK
4d
Everyone's eating filled blocks now—and here's a winner covered with milk chocolate

½ lb. PEPPERMINT CREMES
9d
Beautifully smooth—and the flavour is a delight

MILK TURKISH DELIGHT
2d
Really luscious—try it!

MILK ALMOND WHIRLS
6d
PER QTR.
The crispest of nuts—the milkiest of chocolate (Also Plain if preferred)

FRUIT DELIGHTS (MILK COVERED)
4d
PER QTR.
You can taste the fruit flavours—juicy and fresh

MILK COFFEE BLOCK
2d
Cadburys Chocolate, with a coffee flavour! The biggest taste thrill for years

CADBURYS OF BOURNVILLE *The Factory in a Garden*

OTHER PRICES

Bungalow - Near Brighton & Worthing (freehold)	£499
Triumph Dolomite Roadster Coupe 2l Car	£450
Wolseley Luxury Ten Car (including tax)	£222.10s
Gamage Motor Oil (5 gallons)	12s.6d
Gamage De Luxe Bicycle	£5.19s.6d
Old Hall Holiday Camp, Great Yarmouth (7 days)	£2.5s
ABC Indoor Air Raid Shelter	£5.5s
3 Piece Suite	9½gns
66 Piece Dinner Service	£1.10s
5 Drawer Tallboy	14s.9d
Enamelled Top Table Cupboard	17s.11d
Extra Strong Underbed Wardrobe Or Toy Chest	10s
Somerset Spring Interior 4ft 6in Mattress	£2.5s.6d
Superior 5ft Slate Bed Billiard Table	£5.3s
Darts Outfit Board & Cabinet	£1
Whiteley's 8 Valve Push Pull Radiogram	12½gns
Radio Rentals 'Rent Your Radio' (per week)	1s.9d
Reconditioned Electrolux Vacuum Cleaner	£5.15s
Goblin Wizard Reconditioned Cleaner	£1.17s.6d
Infra-Red & Radiant Heat Lamp	£1.19s.6d
Mottle Axminster Carpet (square yard)	4s.9d
Kodak Popular Brownie Camera	5s.6d
Longchamp 8x Prism Binoculars	£2.15s
Bavingtons Mens Stainless Steel Westrista Watch	£3.10s
Bavingtons Ladies Dainty Nickel Chromium Watch	£1.2s.6d
Goya Original Ladies Perfume	3s

The Triumph Dolomite Roadster Coupe. Class winner in the recent R.A.C. and Scottish Rallies. Prices, including discs and full equipment, £395 for the 14/65, and £450 for the two-litre.

TRIUMPH COMPANY, LTD., COVENTRY. London Showrooms: 28, ALBEMARLE STREET., W.1.

CIGARETTES

A SIMPLE EQUATION

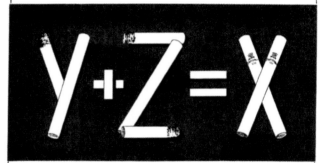

$$Y \div Z = X$$

Which you can prove for yourself

Problem: To determine the best value obtainable in cigarettes.

Solution: Let Y = Number of cigarettes, Z = the price, and X = the best value for money. Then Y + Z = X. Frankly we started this little problem hopefully, but the solution is not so easy. Unless it is known that Y = 10 and Z = 6½d. then, of course, it is being proved by thousands every day that

X = 333 (State Express Three Threes)

Three Threes
STATE EXPRESS 333
10 for 6½ᴰ

---

10 minutes to wait so....

Mine's a MINOR

De Reszke - of course!

10 FOR 5ᴰ   15 FOR 7½ᴰ   20 FOR 10ᴰ   30 FOR 1'3

Sent DUTY FREE to members of the B.E.F. in France: 120 for 2'-, 240 for 4'-. Postage 9d. Order through your tobacconist.

K 4's

10 for 6ᵈ EVEN

Finest Value in Virginia 10's

Also 4 and 20 — 1ˢ 2ᵈ

Join the Navy in smoking *Ardath* **STRAIGHT CUT**
The Navy's Favourite Cigarette

So tremendously popular in the Navy and overseas, Straight Cut is now available to you. Note the price - 6d. for 10 - and try a packet to-day.

10 for 6ᴰ

120 STRAIGHT CUT may be sent DUTY FREE to H.M. Navy and B.E.F. for 3/2, postage paid.

Craven "A"
for your throats sake!

THERE is a touch of quality about Craven 'A' that you will appreciate at once. And these cork-tipped cigarettes are consistently satisfying because they are made to an unvarying standard of excellence. Smoke as many as you will — you can rely on the fact that they never affect the throat.

10 for 7d · 20 for 1/2

MADE SPECIALLY TO PREVENT SORE THROATS

CURRENCY

Money Conversion Table

Old Money		Equivalent Today
Farthing	¼d	0.1p
Half Penny	½d	0.21p
Penny	1d	0.42p
Threepence	3d	1.25p
Sixpence	6d	2.5p
Shilling	1s	5p
Florin	2s	10p
Half Crown	2s 6d	12.5p
Crown	5s	25p
Ten Shillings	10s	50p
Pound	20s	£1
Guinea	21s	£1.05

CARTOONS

King Swee'pea

Jane . . .

The Ruggles Family

PIP, SQUEAK AND WILFRED

KILLING TIME!

Printed in Great
Britain
by Amazon